The Blue Nib
Chapbook 2

Winter/Spring Chapbook Contest 2017/18

1st: Anne Walsh Donnelly
2nd: Akshaya Pawaskar
3rd: Bobbie Sparrow

Edited by Shirley Bell

The Blue Nib
Chapbook 2
Winter/Spring Chapbook Contest 2017/18

First published in Great Britain in 2018 by The Blue Nib

Copyright © The Blue Nib

The rights of
Anne Walsh Donnelly, Akshaya Pawaskar
and Bobbie Sparrow to be identified
as the authors of this work has been asserted by them in
accordance with the
Copyright, Design and Patents Act of 1988
All rights reserved

ISBN: 978-1-9999550-4-5

Table of Contents

WINTER/SPRING Chapbook Contest 2017/2018 1

Winners: 3

Introduction 5

JUDGE'S REPORT 7

1st: Anne Walsh Donnelly 9

An Irish Wake 11

Odd As Fuck. Conversation overheard in a rural post office, 13th February, 1988 13

Prayers after Communion 15

Friesian 17

Bitter Guinness 18

Bailey 19

Tawny Owl 20

The Last Dance 21

2nd: Akshaya Pawaskar 23

Ekphrasis 25

Stabbed with a nib 27

Winter returning 29

I do 31

Mutant 32

Forget me not 34

Stockholm syndrome 36

Inked 38

3rd: Bobbie Sparrow 41
Surrender 43
Badger 45
The worn ego 46
Father 47
Eve's legacy 49
Brother Conall's active prayer 51
Death of a windmill 53
Descent 54
Biographies: 56

WINTER/SPRING Chapbook Contest 2017/2018

3 poets/24 poems/1 chapbook

1st Prize: $150; 2nd Prize :$100.00 3rd Prize $50.00

3 winning poets will have their work included in the chapbook

RULES

The competition is open to new, emerging and established poets from any country BUT at least one of the three winners will be a debutante (with no chapbook or book published previously). Up to 10 other entrants will be listed as "highly commended".

Entries must consist of 8 poems, in the English language and the sole work of the entrant with no translations or 'versions'. The poems can be in verse or prose. Entries must be work not previously published by The Blue Nib.

JUDGED BY

KEVIN HIGGINS

Winners:

WINNER Anne Walsh Donnelly (debutante)
SECOND PLACE Akshaya Pawaskar (debutante)
THIRD PLACE Bobbie Sparrow (debutante)

Introduction

Welcome to the Blue Nib's second chapbook, which showcases the prize- winning entries to our second Chapbook Contest, The Winter/Spring Chapbook Contest, 2017/18. The Blue Nib is a not for profit small press and online publishing platform run by editors Shirley Bell & Dave Kavanagh.

In The Blue Nib magazine we offered the 3 winning poets, in first, second and third places, chapbook publication, along with cash prizes and their copies of this chapbook. The contest was open to new, emerging and established poets from any country but at least one of the three winners was to be a debutante (with no chapbook or book published previously). Again, we were delighted to find that all three winners were debutantes, so we are proud to be the first publisher to introduce these new poets into print.

We are introducing three very strong female writers, all writing with passion and conviction, but all having their own very distinctive voices.

Our judge was the fine Irish poet, Kevin Higgins. (See his biography at the end of the chapbook).

We are very pleased to be able to showcase these emerging talents.

Shirley Bell and Dave Kavanagh
The Blue Nib
July 2018
www.magazine.thebluenib.com

JUDGE'S REPORT

I was impressed by the generally high standard of the entries. So many lively and witty and sad and clever poems, all speaking in their own essential voice. Every poet whose work I read here had something to offer, and potential. The ten poets who receive Honourable Mention are all clearly profoundly serious about the art of poetry and, crucially, they manage to combine that seriousness with an ability to have fun writing poems; at least that's how it seemed to this reader. The top three placed poets soared a little above the other entries in that their poems had a consistent quality; every poem had something excellent about it. The winner is a poet of exceptional bravery, a pretty sensational original voice. I hope the poetry world doesn't tame her, though no doubt it will try.

Kevin Higgins, 8-5-2018

1st: Anne Walsh Donnelly

An Irish Wake

You'd never leave him stuck for a pint
even though he'd be out draining
the spuds when it was his round.

You could always rely on Jack
to give a hand when you'd be saving the hay.
Has my baler for the last year
every time I asked him to leave it back
he'd promise he would, first thing the next day.

The best midfielder we ever had,
we'd never have won the county championship
without him. Remember the time
he scored a point from the seventy yard line,
then punched the other team's full forward,
knocked him unconscious.

Always seen in the florist's shop
on Valentine's day buying roses for the wife,
every Valentine's night in the pub
arms around some young wan
out for the ride.

Didn't he produce a strapping son?
Brilliant midfielder too.
I remember the day he was born
Jack went on the beer for a week.

Took him out of school
when he was sixteen to help with the farm.
Look at the buck now,
poteen face on him,
sure anyone drinking a lug of that stuff
would be yelping like a lost puppy.

And Jack's wife beside the coffin
bawling her eyes out.
I'd say she was slicing onions all day.

I'll call over tomorrow after the burial
to collect my machine.

Odd As Fuck. Conversation overheard in a rural post office, 13th February, 1988

Bridie, did I tell you, Victoria dyed her hair,
same colour as a hawthorn berry?
I nearly choked on the Body of Christ
when she knelt beside me at the altar on Sunday.

And she's taken up writing.
Had a poem in the Mayo Tribune last week.
I knew the day herself and Jim
got married it wouldn't last. Dancing

like a goat up the aisle, no father
to give her away, no proper hymns at the Mass,
just some of that Chris De Burgh shite
all the young wans are into these days.

Wore a purple velvet dress,
rainbow ear rings and as for her five brothers.
They were the bridesmaids.
As himself said, "odd as fuck."

Anyway a girl like her shouldn't be wearing white.
I told Jim, she didn't save herself for him.
And do you know what he said to me?
Ma, the only virgins in this town are the nuns.

Paid no heed to my warnings.
I know sons never do. Think us mammies are eejits.
Not an eejit now he's back in his own bedroom,
waking up to the smell of a fry every morning.

She wasn't very domesticated either. I could smell
the steak burning from our house.
Every sponge cake,
she made in that fancy new range collapsed.

God only knows what kind of off-spring she'd have produced.
And she wouldn't be the type of woman
that'd mind himself and meself in our old age.
Not that I'd want her wiping my arse when the time comes.

Wasn't it awful sad about Dick Hanley?
Only 69. Maggie will find it hard to manage the farm
on her own. I hear her daughter's moving home
from Dublin, got a teaching job in Ballina.

She'll be on the hunt for a man.
A laying hen like her will have no bother getting one.
Bridie, did I tell you? Jim's applied for an annulment.
I'm posting his application now.

Prayers after Communion

(i)
God, would ya make it okay to be gay?
Or strike Jack Doyle dumb.
Stop him calling me a "shirt-lifter."

Would ya give me A's in my Leaving Cert?
So I can get away from me Ma,
Da and squealing bonhams.

Would ya forgive me if I went to confess
me sins and rode Fr. Murphy in the box?
I'd say a hundred decades of the rosary, after.

Would ya let me join the seminary,
if I fail the Leaving?
I'd look good in white vestments.

(ii)
Dear God, please don't let me kill my husband.
Stood over the bed last night with the bread knife.
I'd have cut his nose off, only for the baby crying.
I can't cope with those Guinness snores.

Doc says if I take some tablets I won't be as jittery.
Says women get a bit down after having a baby.
Down, me arse. I love babies.
I want another, but husband won't come near me.

Says he'll only go in covered.
His cousin's coming home from London
at Christmas, with a case full of condoms.
Says I'll have to wait till then.

That's months away.
And the killer is –
he's great at making babies.
Knows exactly how to get me going.

(iii)
Oh my God, the wife nearly killed me last night.
Worst nightmare I've ever had.
When I woke up she was in the bed beside me feeding the baby.

And now she wants another one. As if thirteen wasn't enough.
I'm afraid to go near her in case she gets pregnant again.
Have to go to the bathroom to get relief.

God, would you take the notion
of wanting more kids out of her head? Doc
says he'll prescribe the pill on medical grounds.

(iv)
Dear Heavenly Father, would you give a special blessing
to the husband and wife in the front row.
They both look wretched. It must be very difficult

for them, trying to raise all those children.
Would you make sure their young buck,
the one with the tight jeans does well in his exams

and send him off to Dublin?
It's very hard to say Mass
when he's looking at me with his dog-in-heat eyes

and long fingers playing piano on his crotch.
I have to lock the door of the confessional box
when I see him coming for absolution.

Friesian

The new vet's perfume
cut through the shite in the shed.
She pulled on shoulder-length gloves,
reached inside my best dairy cow

up through the birth canal.
The animal roared like a chainsaw
until in a whoosh of blood,
a Friesian calf slipped out.

After the calf had suckled
I asked the new vet in for tea,
released my copper highlighted hair
from its pony tail while she washed.

The first time we made love
her hands delivered me from my labour.
Like my Friesian calf, I landed
on sweet-smelling straw.

Bitter Guinness

I slurp dregs, immune to bitterness.
Murder cigarette.
Fumble in jeans pocket
for my last coins,
throw them on the counter,
nod at barman.
He pulls another pint.

I swipe my phone. She smiles,
we walk by Cliffs of Moher.
Grind knuckles in sockets.
Why haven't I changed my screen saver?

Grab fresh Guinness,
head not fully settled.
Gulp. Sneeze, splutter, splash,
down my creased shirt.

"Are you sorry?" she asked,
on the steps of courthouse
yesterday. I dug my toe into a crack
prised apart by clumps of dandelions.

"For what?"

Forehead creased, she flinched
as a cop car blared past.
I wanted to take her in my arms.

"You're the one who walked,"
I said. Glared at the porter,
as he locked the courthouse doors.

"Yes, but you left me years before
I gave up on us."

Bailey

I stare through the jagged glass hole
in the window pane, green ferns
around my cottage are blood splattered.
I flop into my armchair, try to remember.

Bailey's paws plod on kitchen tiles,
his wet nose nudges, his anxious eyes
beg me for a walk. I try to catch the familiar
smell of burning peat and his bushy odour.

He opens his mouth, no sound.
Haven't heard a bark since
last winter. I buried him under
the pear tree in the orchard.

He circles the kitchen, makes me
dizzy. Through his golden blur, I see
an elderly woman on the floor.
She wears my polka dotted apron,

dusted with flour, ladder in nude tights
on her right thigh, just like the one
my thumb made this morning
when getting dressed.

I notice the broken chair, upturned
pine dresser and all my willow-pattern plates
in pieces. I run out the back door, towards
the ferns, to see if my blood's splattered

there. Waiting on the fronds, a cortege
of ladybirds. Bailey pushes his hefty body
against my legs. The ladybirds alight
and helicopter in the air.

Tawny Owl

Each night after my husband fell asleep
and the moon was full
I'd gaze from the bedroom window
at the tawny owl
perched on the barn's roof.

I'd move a hand up my thigh,
dream of laying my head
on her feathered mound.

I'd move my other hand,
down my arched neck,
dream of holding her breast
in my palm, her breath,
moistening my desert skin.

Sometimes I opened the window to listen
to her melody of "Tu-woo's,"
before husband shoved himself inside me.

In daylight I milked cows,
pulled eggs from bottoms of stubborn hens,
fed motherless lambs.

One November morning
I found my owl,
her limp body,
floating face down
in the duck pond.
I cawed like an old crow.

The Last Dance

Jack leans against the concrete wall
scrutinises the Hereford Heifer standing in the ring
she excretes onto sawdust. He sneezes
wonders how much she might cost
how many calves she'd produce.
More than the woman he could have married?

Bidding starts slow
herds of farmers hide their eyes
behind curtains of nonchalance.
Jack fingers the hundred-pound notes in his pocket
bidding escalates. He waits
the auctioneer's voice spirals upwards
his hammer suspended mid-air

Jack starts to raise his hand, the heifer bellows
as her handler pokes her hindquarters with a stick
Jack falters. The hammer falls, a cattle trader
from the North roars like a victorious Viking.

Jack bangs shut his kitchen door
cash still lodged in his pockets
slumps into the fireside chair
stares at ash on the grate
stomach like an active volcano.
He unbuckles his belt,

remembers the night in the town hall
when he lumbered towards the only girl
in the county, worth her dowry,
remembers an English buck jump
into the space between them
and pull her to the floor
for the last dance.

2nd: Akshaya Pawaskar

Ekphrasis

L'art pour l'art on
the whitewashed walls
come to life like dolls

And talk in haunting tongue

They are just like us

Seldom understood

However voluble,

Cryptic in between

The strokes, chiaroscuro.

The abstract all left
to the poet to repaint

On blanker sheets with

Wernicke's area firing

Away like blitz

Only it rains ink

Centripetal, the motion

Of colors.

Till they fuse.

The doll transforms

Into a white stallion

Greek in pedigree
And the thunk of
His hooves
welcomes
The fountain of
Hippocrene on this

Turf eons away

From Mount Helicon

Oh Pegasus friend of muses
A winged verse
You fly, you fly

Stabbed with a nib

You cannot silence her at gun point. How can

you, when she has already opened your

body full of fluted skeletons

from her bear hug. They grin from within you.
What goes around doesn't wander

too far, gravitating back

She talks in silence, subtle and lucid. Sonorous

Lines spit her sophisticated wrath

In black and white

The Pen is mightier than the Sword so save

the latter for another era to chop off

your hangdog crown.

You were the entire draft of her debut Novel

until you were redacted piecemeal to

a paltry chapter.

Hell hath no fury like a pen wielded by a scorned woman. But you didn't think it twice over in
 your Mice brain and

Now she killed you with her insolent snakefanged nib. Bonsaied from a panthera to a bay cat, feeling endangered,

You don't haunt her anymore. Her purging on

the leaf, portentous contaminates you
With Consumption.

Winter returning

The vinyl rotating on the turntable

Transforms the mute monochrome color

Blue, not of spring skies but

Of cyanosed lips.

The languid soft purr is deafening
more than the loud babel of mocking bird

It trespasses under my skin
Beetles crawling.

Sunshine is swaddled in sea-haar
and the quietude is quite disquieting
its upheaval so oxymoronic
Cohabiting in a body

Barrenness of the still season echoes
grandfather-clocklike in a room that is

Abandoned for lack of an inglenook

Surfeit of broken panes

The six sided angels don't elate when

placed on the tongue to be swallowed

as snow treats. This winter of mind
is wintrier than poles.

I do

The white bride walked
Down the aisle and looked
in the pew, where all friends
She thought she would
see. Instead there stood
Heads of Rapa Nui.

The groom was ghost of
her past dressed in black of
darkest hue where light could
not spark a shine, even on
the rich vestment
clashing new.

She did not see the priest,
till last with eyes wetted on
her plight that she was
widow of the dead, defunct
future that she was
About to wed.

Mutant

Amino acid chains to nucleotides
to double helix DNA to genetics and

probabilities.
And the chaotic mess emerges
Like a mutant damaged but unique
Unique but lost
Like she belongs to the lost generation
Anachronistic and out of place, always
Coloring outside lines
Like a child, hedonistic expressive, war
Ravaged yet never felt the cold metal
Nor witnessed blitz
She could fit in at the several cafes on
The Montparnasse or be seen cavorting
On the banks of seine
But she is now and here stuck in this era,

Materialistic, and her rabbit hole Paris,
ghost of its older self
And her literature not belonging to any
Genre her musical tastes, un jazz like
Growing wintrier.

She waits to time travel and waits until

she is frozen in that stance until her wait

weighs her down to
Amino acid chains to nucleotides
to double helix DNA to genetics and

probabilities and dust.

Forget me not

    Wearer will not be forgotten
    she read it somewhere so
    She tucked a forget me not
    Behind her ear
    Waiting for her lover
    She was holding the torch
    But the ship had sailed
    As she watched and
    So did the yellow eye of
    Mouse eared flower and
    It went bluer than it
    Was blue
    Pulling a fig over
    her heart congested with
    One sided shameless
    Love
    Pulling a fig over the fat
    Blob, salty near the rim of
    The socket holding globe
    Of the eye
    She took a pestle and
    Crushed the gimcrack
    Petal after petal bestowing
    On them label

Unfaithful, now they adorn her
wilderness and every sigh
of wind carries their whisper
to her ears,
'The myth is a big fat lie'.

Stockholm syndrome

    You tried to lift your head
    and you could not see it
    Fuseli's gremlin was
    Out of your sight yet
    you searched, frantic.
    Body limp but you could
    Feel a phantom limb
    Move all in your head
    You saw yourself wandering
    out of your home and
    the body housing
    your soul was immobile
    Its roots in your bed
    And over your limbs
    Like sinews and your
    Breathing labored
    As when underwater
    The ocean beats and
    Fits around your chest
    Like a tight corset.
    And the prince is
    a gremlin sitting on
    your chest to pull it
    Tighter and how
    unhealthy you felt as
    you missed him when

He stood you up.
Trapped in a dead
Body, an alive soul.
This feeling of disgust
Stockholm syndrome.

Inked

That quaver on my back
came to life as I bled,
ever so slightly.
But bore the needling pain
As the sewing machine
stitched,
A patch over my pale skin
and made it indigo black
and rain washed
My demure image and made
it into rebel. Here I stood
with the same
Face but the value had cart
Wheeled. I was the same girl
But now I had
been the one tainted with ink.
The ink that shaped my words
indecipherable

Inaudible as they were unuttered.
They took a form of poem and
spoke loudly like the
Wailing wind and crashing
waves and the quaver on my back
sang and smiled at my
Backbiters and rendered them
toothless. Yes I was loud,
as loud as they come.

3rd: Bobbie Sparrow

Surrender

when I am full of the world's noise
I go to the fields to empty myself
I lie and ask the sky
what must my breath expel?

a cerulean blue lifts my blindness
a white cloud is a distant chaos
each spun out thread
a brokenness against the whole

the sun asks joy of me but I am mute
in quiet I sense the certainty of rain
which will sedate the birds
who call my name

at night the fields are mine
the moon reflects my diminished self
I wait for stars   each one   I think
a flickering love note from the dead

can grief shine?   if it does
I lie in dark grass offering
the expanse of me to the heavens
all ambition surrendered to the soil

I breathe in imperfection
its luminosity my torch
so I might see the great mystery
naked and unguarded

Badger
After Henry Scott-Holland

Death is nothing at all

you have only slipped away

a still brush of wild

slain

by the rush of the tamed.

Your small heart's work

is ceased

while the asphalt receives

your blood

your life rises high above the N84

looking down you think

So that

is a badger.

The worn ego

The rook   the alder   the eye
drawn up   away
from these earth soiled feet,
shook from the damp past.
Throat opens to call in the clouds,
shape shift the sky to easy blue.
Hands gently cleave a fontanel in white
heels rise to step into a new world.

A deep ache recalls
your wingless self   bound
to a path   a way.
The work world calls but
spoken words are dry sticks,
crutches to lurch through the day.

How hard it is   to carry
the tired body with grace
kneel   watch
the ant in tiny canter
across the army of grass
blind to the sky but awake with intent.

Father

I see you at the corner
a glimpse from my blind side
that pulls me forward   I lunge
grief as my spur
only to see another man
with your hair   walk away

the longing is a virus taking me down

I hear you one evening
your feet on the gravel   coming home
the promise of your key in the lock
then the rush of grief's river
roaring in my ears
next   silence thumping my temples

I lie down to sleep it away

I cry out to you one night
a creature's howl   my body
cannot contain
it soars from me   beats me with its wings

grief in purple bruises
skin afraid of light

I feel a fracture in my brain

I am a fast falling Alice
no space to look or touch   no white rabbit
just a hurtling vault
from some other horizon   until
as suddenly as you went
I become   a smaller me

I feel time collapsing

I should have leaned into the pain
but I didn't know how
        only nineteen
the world outside opening its arms
but no one to clothe me
wearing only the hood of grief

I yearned for you to lead me out

Eve's legacy

She thinks when we die we return
to the earth   I believed her
thought of apples hidden in the grass
their bruised under bellies letting go.
If I had picked that Beauty of Bath
in time   I could have felt its moment of perfection
in my soft mouth   the final sweetness
a heaven in itself   and yet perhaps
the moment just before   when tongue expects
what apple promises   would raise me up.

The lovers on Keats' urn are painted into
this eternal arousal but I am alive
must seek paradise in present pleasures.
The ripe plum   skin surprised by teeth
my lips a purple smile   for she is easy,
a willing corruptor with flesh that yields.
The orange demands to be undressed
needs nails splitting pith   bites
to penetrate a hundred tiny corpuscles of juice.
She needs a mouth with purpose   divine

retribution is found in the berry   blooded
cloak most pleasing to view   tiny eyes
in the straw reflecting a heart
the birds may pick before my eager fingers.
Raspberry   Logan   Black   Blue
four orchestral movements
conducted by the sun
who raises them from womb to mouth,
the lyric shining to the blind.

Brother Conall's active prayer
September 1598

The river is in her ninth month

water broken, the grass lapping.

Wilted whispers turn to moist surrender,

I slip in with the eels

shoes upon my head

my heart a swell in the throat.

The cold does not halt my urge.

When the moon is too bright

I swim where the water curls the reeds,

debris of the day thwarted by dark clay.

My arms are unsure,

the river has its own night ease

trees speak to the pebbles beneath,

I interrupt their parley.

Listen, a cormorant's wings are the small thunder of my fear.

I see soldiers spread on our walls

King Henry is the spell that plunders

sacred space, expulsing men who pray.

But we are Machiavellian monks,
God hears us from the scrub.
Like the thrush, we are brown but glorious.
My body agitates the soil
still swimming, cloister side.

Stone has its own story
my hands touch grey notch and jag
words to a blind man, darkness
is known   but steel is not.
I cannot see the blood but hear
the jubilant archer's cry.
My eyes close on the sight of the cross.

Listen, a cormorant's wings are the small thunder of my release.

Death of a windmill

That day was wet and still
my heart already sore.
His arms were thrown apart,
calling upon a large God
blades dug into the stubborn soil.
I knelt to place my palm on cold flank,
the white in his stand
had turned grey in his fall.

Where was his command
his capture of the clouds,
the echoes of whipped song
arresting the walker's ear.
How could we bury this giant?
No hymn would be loud enough,
no shoulders would suffice.

We are nothing to him now
and he is immaterial without the wind.

Descent

*One does not become enlightened by imagining figures of
light, but by making the darkness conscious.* —Carl Jung

Step into your body

Give thanks

Catch the vapours of the brain
in a silver censer for blessing.
Weave about the throat
hearing the orchestra of voices
from piccolo to double bass.

Give thanks

Quietly orbit the heart
listen to the murmur:

Sometimes I am a thousand petalled lotus
Sometimes I am a bruise

Breathe in the lung
surrender to your grief   fall
into the belly   full
of elements

Give thanks

Be curious of viscid despair,
there is no weight without shadow.
Climb on Persephone's swing,
waist to womb   navel to pudenda.

Give thanks

Your lower self will resurrect you.
Stretch out to the skin;
where the rivers of blood meet the world
your coagulated being rises.
Now see with new eyes
carry burdens with changed hands.
Your creation begins again.

Biographies:

Chapbook Judge, Kevin Higgins

Kevin Higgins is co-organiser of Over The Edge literary events. He teaches poetry workshops at Galway Arts Centre, Creative Writing at Galway Technical Institute, and is Creative Writing Director for the NUI Galway Summer School.
He is poetry critic of *The Galway Advertiser*. His poetry is discussed in *The Cambridge Introduction to Modern Irish Poetry* and features in the generation defining anthology *Identity Parade –New British and Irish Poets* (Ed. Roddy Lumsden, Bloodaxe, 2010) and in *The Hundred Years' War: modern war poems* (Ed. Neil Astley, Bloodaxe, April 2014).
Kevin's poetry has been translated into Greek, Spanish, Italian, Japanese, Russian, & Portuguese. In 2014 Kevin's poetry was the subject of a paper 'The Case of Kevin Higgins, or, 'The Present State of Irish Poetic Satire' presented by David Wheatley at a Symposium on Satire at the University of Aberdeen.
He was Satirist-in-Residence at the Bogman's Cannon (2015-16). '2016 – The Selected Satires of Kevin Higgins' was published by NuaScéalta in early 2016. A pamphlet of Kevin's political poems *The Minister For Poetry Has Decreed* was published last December by the Culture Matters imprint of the UK based Manifesto Press. His poems have been praised by, among others, Tony Blair's biographer John Rentoul, *Observer* columnist Nick Cohen, and *Sunday Independent* columnist Gene Kerrigan; and have been quoted in *The Daily Telegraph*, *The Times* (UK), *The Independent*, and *The Daily Mirror*.

The Stinging Fly magazine recently described Kevin as "likely the most read living poet in Ireland." *Song of Songs 2.0: New & Selected Poems* was published earlier this year by Salmon and includes a substantial number of new poems as well as selections from his six previous poetry collections.

Anne Walsh Donnelly lives in Castlebar, Co. Mayo. Her work has been published in various literary magazines such as Crannog, Boyne Berries, The Blue Nib, Star82 Review and Cold Coffee Stand. Her short stories have been shortlisted in competitions such as the OTE New Writer of the Year Award (2014, 2016), Fish International Prize (2015) and the RTE Radio One Frances Mac Manus competition (2014, 2015). One of her poems was highly commended in the OTE New Writer of the Year Award (2017), another commended in the Westport Arts Festival poetry competition (2017). She was placed third in the OTE culture night poetry open mic in 2017.

Akshaya Pawaskar is a doctor practicing in India and poetry is her passion. Her poems have been published in Tipton Poetry journal, Writer's Ezine, Efiction India, Ink drift, The Blue Nib, Her heart poetry, Awake in the world anthology by Riverfeet press and a few anthologies by lost tower publications. She has been chosen as 'Poet of the week' on Poetry superhighway and was featured writer in Wordweavers poetry contest.

Bobbie Sparrow is a poetry writing psychotherapist. Her poems have been published in both national and international journals including *Orbis, Crannog, Picaroon* and *Skylight 47*. Her work has been translated into Italian for *Inkroci* magazine. Bobbie was the Featured reader at the Over The Edge open Mic August 2017 and will be a featured reader at the Far From event in Cuírt 2018. She lives on the shores of Lough Corrib, Co. Galway, Ireland with her husband and their two fine sons. Bobbie finds a good poem to be a good friend.